RELATIONSHIP SCHOOL

A PATH OF CONSCIOUS LOVING

DR. RICHARD JORDAN

Old Mountain Press

RELATIONSHIP SCHOOL

A PATH OF CONSCIOUS LOVING

INCLUDES A POWERFUL WAY TO STOP ARGUMENTS IN SECONDS

In less than two hours this book will help you understand your relationships and provide tools to create more loving.

Published by:
Old Mountain Press, Inc.
2542 S. Edgewater Dr.
Fayetteville, NC 28303

www.oldmp.com

© 1999 Dr. Richard Jordan

ISBN: 1-884778-63-1
Library of Congress Catalog Card Number: 99-61241

Relationship School: A Path of Conscious Loving.

First Edition
Manufactured in the United States of America
1 2 3 4 5 6 7 8 9 10

Acknowledgments

This book is based upon what I have learned from many teachers and what I have experienced thus far. I especially acknowledge Drs. Ron and Mary Hulnick at the University of Santa Monica and Drs. Gay and Kathlyn Hendricks at the Hendricks Institute. Much of the information in this book reflects their teachings.

I thank those who reviewed the book and graciously provided input, including Dr. Gay Hendricks, Dr. Jane Myers Drew, Dr. Marcie Jenner, Cheryl Medicine Song, Debra Lanae Hampton, Pat and Charles Hampton, and Dr. Barbara Whitaker.

I am deeply grateful for all my other teachers, collaborators, and partners, and for the couples with whom I work. I continue to learn from each of you.

CONTENTS

INTRODUCTION

School? Yuck! Why write a book about school? Most of us remember school as sitting in rows with a teacher who often would rather be doing something else. School was about learning to do things a certain prescribed way, the right way. School convinced many of us that we weren't very creative at all. School taught us how to forget our essence.

I remember a time in about the fifth grade when I had finished an in-class assignment quickly, was sitting quietly, and the teacher asked me what I was doing. I responded, "I'm thinking." The teacher was not very happy with that answer. If your school was like mine, they should have called it The School of Embarrassment and Performance Anxiety.

In spite of all this, I risk your alienation by using the term Relationship School. I do this because I believe it is such a powerful metaphor. If you are breathing right now, you are enrolled in the University of Life. In the University of Life, Relationship School offers a kind of sub-curriculum that is practically unavoidable unless you are a hermit. So, the way I look at it, you might as well show up for the lessons because they are going to be presented to you anyway.

In Relationship School you are invited and encouraged to be creative and to have as much fun as you can! In fact, if you learn the lessons well, you *will* have fun, creative expression, and an abundance of loving. When all is said and done, this is the real school. That other school was just an unfortunate by-product of our culture.

One reason I wrote this book is to save time in therapy. I have found that much of the early work with couples involves finding a way of talking about relationships that makes sense, assisting them in getting clear about just what is going on, and getting clear about what they want to manifest together. It seems to me that the essence of this process is quite similar among most couples.

While each person and each couple is unique, there seem to be many things in common. Some things also seem to be universal. For example, each of us yearns to be intimate, and each of us fears it. So relationship becomes a dance between our fears and our longing for connection, a "tension of the opposites."

So, I thought, "Wouldn't it be great if there were some way to distill the essence and provide it in a clear way that could be easily read and understood in only an hour or two?" It certainly would not answer all questions, but it might cause us to think and help give us a common language with which to enter the rocky shoals of relationship therapy, where great treasure is often found.

This book is also useful for people who simply want to better understand themselves and their partners in relationship. It can be used as a foundation from which to work your own process, whatever that may be for you. Or you may simply want to talk with your partner about whatever you find in this book that stimulates you, which may help you develop a deeper awareness of the rich landscape of relationship that you are sharing.

WHAT HAPPENED?

"Though love is gentle and love is kind
The sweetest flower when first it's new
But love grows old and waxes cold
And fades away like morning dew."
from The Water is Wide
Irish traditional song

I enjoy hearing stories of how couples met. Perhaps their eyes met across a crowded room and they felt inexorably drawn to one another. Or maybe they just happened to sit next to each other on a long plane flight, began talking, decided to stay in contact, and.....well, you know. They may have been friends for years and suddenly one quiet evening, on the sofa innocently watching a video, they fell in love. There are as many varieties of this story of romance as there are snowflakes, and couples almost always talk about this time in their relationships with great fondness.

That spark of attraction and the energy of romance we experience in the initial stages are precious and important. They provide the momentum that draws us close. Later in relationship, remembering and re-awakening those initial feelings can provide a touchstone, a reminder of the energy of your initial bond, and a rich source of "juice" and fun.

The problem with romance is this. For various reasons, that initial energy of attraction will diminish as the relationship progresses. "But wait a minute," you say. "I thought this one was the real thing!" And if it is the real thing, this magic feeling should last forever. Or so we have been led to believe. So when it begins to change, you begin to doubt your partner, yourself. You begin to get glimpses of your partner as the real human being on the other side of the veil – that veil you have woven to only allow you to see the image of your ideal partner. Now, the easy part of the relationship is over. Some would say this is where the real relationship begins.

To help understand our experience of the first few months of a new relationship, I invite you to see it as being powered by a combination of biology, culture, and psyche.

BIOLOGY

The mythical term for our biological sexual attraction is Eros. Eros was the Greek god who was thought to give us sexual desire. Biologically, we are designed and programmed to be sexually attracted to one another for the purpose of making more human beings. Well, how long does that take? A few weeks to a few months perhaps, depending on whether the father stays around long enough to make sure the mother and child are off to a safe start.

Some species are programmed to mate for life, but not us. The chemicals that course through our veins, drawing us together with a seemingly irresistible pull, begin to wear off in a few months. When this happens to other species, they simply move on, or re-enter the herd until the next mating season. And depending upon our own social/cultural setting, some of us do the same thing. But most of us feel compelled by some force other than chemistry to stay.

What makes us stay? We humans exist on at least four levels – our bodies, our thoughts, our feelings, and our souls. These levels are connected and relate to each other in a way that attempts to yield balance or equilibrium. When the biochemistry of attraction shows up on the physical level, our thoughts and feelings are naturally moved to do something with this new and powerful state of affairs. We need to put our strong feelings into some sort of framework that makes sense to our minds. Our culture has provided us with this framework, in the form of the myth of romantic love.

CULTURE

One can actually trace back in history about 900 years to find the "invention" of romantic love. It seems to have started in the Provence region of France, where the nobility were known as "troubadours." They were the first ones in our Western culture to talk of love in the person to person, "I and thou" form, through their poems and music. This was the birth of Amor. Whereas Eros is somewhat impersonal, Amor is very personal.

By now, the idea of romantic love is so ingrained in our psyches that it is like a lens through which we see our relationships. We have been told it is true for so long that it has become truth. Just by being members of our culture, we are automatically "plugged in" to its myths, including those dealing with romantic love. So there is a part of every woman who longs for the Knight in Shining Armor, Prince Charming; and part of every man who longs for the Goddess, the Earth Mother, the Vixen.

The classic stories of romantic love are centuries old or older. Today we are surrounded by their modern-day translations. About half of the songs we hear on the radio are about the deepness and sweetness of that romantic love that we feel early on in relationships. Most of the other songs, especially country/western, are commiserating over that love gone wrong. And then there are the movies, once again idealizing romantic love. And then there are the books, advertising, and….well, you get the picture, we continue to be bombarded with the same centuries-old images of how our relationships should be.

Yes, romantic love is a myth. You may be tempted to stop reading this book now, or even head for the fireplace with it, because your experiences with romantic love have probably been among the juiciest in your life. But wait! I am not suggesting that you turn your back on romance. Enjoy those sweet moments and memories of romantic love, but know that there is more. Calling romantic love a myth does not make it bad. The word "myth" has a bad rap, as any fan of Joseph Campbell can attest. Myths are simply the stories we make up to help make sense of things. They are not lies.

Couples can continue to enjoy the "juiciness" of romantic love so long as they avoid the mistake of thinking that the whole relationship hinges upon maintaining a perpetual state of romance. All the thriving relationships I have seen thus far seem to go through cycles of romance. These couples have learned to honor romance as part of a larger idea of relationship that includes so much more depth, richness, sweetness, and staying power.

I believe the ultimate in relationship is to be able to flow between the three basic levels of relationship: Eros, Amor, and Agape. Eros is the biological, primitive level, like sex on the kitchen table. Amor is a bed full of rose petals on Valentine's Day. Agape is a dedication of the "I and thou" relationship to the Divine, as is done in Tantric practices.

The key to success in this is to become conscious of the roles our psyches play in this process so that romance can be enjoyed from the perspective of the greater whole.

PSYCHE

The word "psyche" is Greek in origin, and translates as either "soul" or "mind." For our purposes right now, let us define the psyche as follows: the sum total of your own unique inner experience of life, including thoughts, feelings, beliefs, dreams, habits, addictions, compulsions, and fears. It includes the part of us that interprets the information our senses take in and causes us to respond in a certain way. Part of it is conscious, and part of it is unconscious. The conscious part consists of what we know that we know, plus what we know that we don't know. The unconscious part consists of what we don't know that we don't know, and this part very powerfully affects our lives.

So the conscious part is what we are aware of, and in being aware, we have the capacity to choose our actions. We consciously choose to act in accordance with what we believe will lead to the best outcome. But for some of us, especially in relationships, we seem to keep getting the same outcomes, and they certainly don't look like what our conscious minds want. This is a big clue that there is something as yet unconscious, something that you don't know that you don't know, that keeps creating these negative outcomes.

One common example of this happens when we experience a parent who leaves the family when we are young. If a girl's father leaves, she may carry information in her unconscious mind that says, "Men leave." So long as this information remains in her unconscious mind, she will tend to create relationships in which men leave.

These unconscious drives, or compulsions, could be running the course of your relationships. And so long as they remain unconscious, you have no choice. No matter how hard you try, no matter how much you resist, the pattern will eventually repeat unless you avoid relationships entirely.

Fortunately, there are ways to solve this problem. We can start by asking three important questions:

How did it get set up this way for me?
How is it working (or not)?
What can I do about it?

HOW DID IT GET SET UP THIS WAY?

Love comes unbidden, can't be forbidden
It takes you and shakes you right down to your shoes
It knows heartache and trial, but accepts no denial
You can't choose who you love, love chooses you.
    Kathy Mattea, from "Love Chooses You"

Each of us has his or her own unique thoughts, feelings, and actions in relationship. The great variable here is the unique makeup of your own personality. Our personality makeup has a lot to do with our early developmental experience in the family. Our early family experiences can affect our lives very powerfully, especially if trauma or abuse was present. But we also frequently see siblings who come from the same traumatic experiences and respond very differently. One sibling might grow up to be very fragile and have great difficulty, whereas another sibling might grow up to be very resilient and successful in all aspects of life. So there are clearly other factors besides family experience that affect who we are.

The three main factors that form your personality are your genetic makeup, your experience in your family of origin, and your experience in the world outside your family (call this environmental). Your genetic makeup is important because it affects how you interpret and respond to your experiences in the world. Your genetic makeup cannot be changed. But when we talk about relationships, your early family experiences are especially important because this is an area we can do something about in present time. We cannot go back in time and change anything, but we can change the way we are within ourselves now. We can do this by bringing awareness and compassion to those difficult or painful past events and how they continue to color our present experience.

Your early family experiences have an effect on how and with whom you enter relationship, and how you conduct yourself within relationship. Simply stated, you are compelled to seek the likeness of your opposite-sex parent. Unless you have already done lots of work around this, you have little choice. It is unconscious. This, of course, assumes that your opposite sex parent was around while you were growing up. If not, the person you seek may be the likeness of some other major person in your early life. It all starts when you are very young.

Beginning in infancy, a boy takes in lots of information about his mother, the sound of her voice, her smell, how she looks, how she relates to him, how she relates to his father, and so on. This becomes a very powerful imprint upon his psyche because, early in life, mother is his main image of Woman.

A similar thing happens for a girl. She takes in her experience of father and this becomes her ideal image of Man. Much of what makes up this ideal image resides in our unconscious minds because much of it is experienced before we have learned to form words or thoughts to go with the experiences.

Some of you might be thinking, "I don't know. My partner doesn't seem anything like my parent." Or, "I think I 'married both of my parents!'" This may indeed be so. One lesson I have learned from my work is that every situation, every relationship, is unique. But remember, because much of your attraction may be based on unconscious compulsion, your conscious mind may struggle to make sense of it. Even so, your ideal inner image of Woman or Man may be made up of ingredients that have nothing to do with your parents.

I can personally attest to this. As I have become more conscious of what makes up my inner image of ideal woman, some aspects seem clearly to come from my experiences with my mother. But the physical appearance of my ideal woman seems less like my mother, but very much like the girlfriend my older brother had when I was ten years old!

I admit that what I have been describing assumes a heterosexual orientation. However, I believe that the same principles apply to those who are attracted to same-sex partners. If this is the case for you, your images and experiences of your same-sex parent or other influential person might have something to do with whom you find attractive.

It is our inner image of the ideal man or woman that provides the energy for those mysterious experiences we have, when your eyes meet, your knees get weak, your heart starts pounding, your voice falters, and so on. It's as if we have finely tuned antennae that can pick up the person among the crowd who elegantly dovetails with us, fits the pattern of our ideal image, or at least fits it enough.

All this could be good news or bad news. To the extent that you experienced your parents in a positive way, you will likely find it easier to re-experience similarly positive relationships. To the extent that your unconscious ideal image is negative, traumatic, or abusive, those negative aspects are lurking in the shadows, waiting for the vehicle of relationship to bring them forth. This may sound like very bad news, but it is not necessarily. With the right attitude and willingness to look, there can be great opportunity here – fertile ground.

HOW IS IT WORKING (or not)?

"It's easy to be enlightened when you're alone."
  Soji

In the beginning when the veil of the ideal image that you are projecting onto your partner is vivid and strong, your partner can do no wrong. But as the initial chemistry fades and you begin to experience your partner as a real human being, "problems" emerge. I think "disillusionment" is a good word to describe what happens. You literally begin to lose your illusions about who you thought your partner was. You might become disheartened, sad, upset, or angry. They fooled you, lied to you, pretended to be someone that they weren't. But consider this: the person you are now wondering if you can live with is the same person you fell in love with.

At this point you can blame one another for what's not working, chalk it up to experience, and try again (likely repeating the same patterns). You can make your partner wrong for not being exactly like your projected ideal image and try again to find "the one." Or you can begin asking questions from a place of wonder instead of blame, try something *totally different*. You can choose to show up for your lessons now and see what the relationship looks like beyond the upset you are now experiencing. If you choose to move on in the midst of your upset, without getting the lessons being presented now, you can fully expect to be presented with the opportunity to learn the same lessons again.

I must make a very important clarification here. Nothing I am saying anywhere in this book is suggesting that you allow yourself to be abused in any way, physically, emotionally, verbally, or sexually. Showing up for your lessons is never about being at the effect of abuse. In fact, one lesson some of you might be presented with is the lesson that leads you to say, "I am no longer willing to be at the effect of this."

So some things are working and some things are not. This is true for all relationships. It becomes a matter of how big is the "working" file and how big is the "not working" file. So first get clear on what is in each file. You can start by each of you making a separate list of "What's working, what I like" and "What's not working, what I don't like." Get together and share your lists. This conversation could be very enlightening, and should be conducted using the Basic Communication Skill described at the end of this book. Also make a special mark beside anything on the list that you are sure you simply cannot accept in continued relationship.

This relationship assessment is important in clarifying "what is" right now. It is very difficult to move from "Point A" toward a more positive way of being in relationship — "Point B" — unless you first get yourself fully at Point A. This may sound like a very rational, logical process, and it is. So make your lists at a time when you are not upset or angry. When we are flooded with emotion it is usually impossible to conduct a logical conversation and arrive at a conscious and responsible conclusion.

Also be aware of any temptation to blame your partner for the items in your "not working" file. It is likely that at least a few of those items are things that you have not yet taken full responsibility for. I will talk more about this later.

WHAT CAN I DO ABOUT IT?

"The significant problems we face cannot be solved at the same level of thinking we were at when we created them."
Albert Einstein

Gather your courage. Look at your lists. Is there anything that you simply cannot accept and which you both agree simply cannot be changed? If so, consider ending your relationship. This may sound cold, but many couples go on and on dancing around these "fatal flaws," afraid to bring them to the light, afraid to be alone, afraid they will never find another partner, afraid to deal with their partner's upset, just afraid. Couples sometimes stay together in spite of agonizingly major "problems" because of this fear. They live in tolerable misery, not daring to risk going for the riches of authentic relationship.

Next, what do you do if you have no fatal flaws but the "not working" list looks as massive as the Dead Sea Scrolls? This is not easy to address without some exploration into the specifics of your situation, but one thing you can do is to consider your relationship as a living thing. It is an entity formed by the energy of two people coming together. Like a plant, it requires fertile soil, cultivation, watering, light, loving attention, and patience. You also need to enjoy the flowers and the fruit, and occasionally trim and prune.

What is the quality of the plant you two have formed? How well have you been caring for your plant? How much energy have you been investing in your relationship? How much of it is positive, how much negative? Considering your answers to these questions, does it make sense that your relationship is in the state it is in? Studies show that there needs to be at least *five times* as much positive versus negative communication and interaction for a relationship to be stable, for your plant to grow and be healthy[1]. What would you estimate your ratio to be? How can you get it where it needs to be?

First, let's make sure your plant is still alive. Again, gather your courage. Some couples have immersed the relationship in so much negativity, anger, and hostility for so long that they have lost hope of ever reviving it. There may not be any fatal flaws, but the heaviness and toxicity of their negativity have killed the plant. If this is true for you, once again, consider ending the relationship. But be careful here. Sometimes hope hides. Carefully explore this before you act. If you have experienced lots of negativity, you have also experienced some amount of life history with each other. It is not something to be flung away lightly. Seek outside guidance if you are not sure. Try asking yourself, "Is this person someone I want to be at my deathbed, the last face I see?" Unless the answer is unequivocally "No," there may still be life in the roots of the relationship.

---

[1] "Why Marriages Succeed or Fail," John Gottman, Ph.D (1994)

One very powerful shift I have seen in seemingly doomed relationships happens when one partner moves out of "againstness" and into loving. This usually occurs when the individual is doing his or her own work in therapy or with a teacher, or perhaps through meditation. In a quantum leap of awareness and compassion, one partner realizes the futility and "psychic weight" of his or her own negativity, takes responsibility for it, and moves into loving on their own and for themselves. What an invitation this is for his or her partner, who often shifts more into loving. One partner's getting off his or her position, surrendering "againstness" in favor of loving, shifts the entire relationship. A wise teacher once said, "I don't need your permission to love you." The person doing the loving reaps great rewards.

So, how do I do this? What do I do about it? The way I propose to move into positive, loving, creative relationship is in the form of the Relationship School Curriculum.

THE CURRICULUM

"In the balloon you are prisoners of the wind, and you go only in the direction of the wind. In life people think they are prisoners of circumstance. But in the balloon, as in life, you can change altitude, and when you change altitude, you change direction. You are not a prisoner anymore."
Bertrand Piccard, Swiss psychiatrist and balloonist

As we live our lives and interact with others, we are presented with the lessons of Relationship School. The more successful we are with these lessons, the more loving and creativity we get to experience. In my experience, those who are most successful at relationships have mastered such things as responsibility, authenticity, forgiveness, and commitment. The "curriculum" provided here is one way to effectively move into relationship mastery. It involves three steps: Non-judgmental Awareness, Vision, and Action.

NON-JUDGMENTAL AWARENESS

"Out beyond ideas of wrongdoing and rightdoing there is a field. I'll meet you there."
Rumi

Awareness is a process of noticing and wondering – What is? How is it working? What am I thinking when this happens? How am I feeling when he says that? What are my underlying assumptions and beliefs? What do I wish to change? In a non-judgmental way we notice ourselves being ourselves and bring wonderment to our experience. We are fully present in the moment, with what is.

When you are having relationship challenges, you are painfully aware that something is not working. Your natural tendency is to try to do something to fix it or have it be different. So, for example, when you saw the passage above about needing five times more positive than negative, you may have had an urge to just start being more positive in relationship. Having such positive intentions can be beneficial, but they will only take you so far unless you do something very important first.

You must bring acceptance to things just as they are right now at "Point A." Release your judgment of your partner, your relationship, yourself. To the extent you judge your partner or yourself in relationship, it is exactly to that extent that you are stuck. Your judgment is like glue. The fact is, your judgments are mistakes. I wish to honor each of your own spiritual perspectives, but offer this for your consideration. Nothing is going on here that does not have the Divine Seal of Approval. From the great altitude of the all-knowing, the natural order and sense of all things is apparent.

One way of looking at this is that spiritually, at the soul level, the concept of right/wrong, good/bad disappears. We are left with choices and consequences, all of which provide us with the opportunity to learn and grow, or else to repeat the lessons. This is not to discount the importance and necessity of moral right and wrong as an essential ingredient of an orderly society. But at the soul level, our judgments of ourselves and others as wrong or bad tend to weigh us down. Consider putting that weight down.

One example of the weight of judgment and its effect on relationships comes from my own experience. When I was eleven years old, the girls in my class got together and made a "slam book." The slam book was a spiral notebook with a boy's name at the top of each page. The girls passed it around, each writing what they thought of each boy. Eventually, of course, the slam book ended up in the hands of us boys. Well, they didn't call it a slam book for nothing. On my page, the girls almost unanimously agreed that I was conceited and egotistical. Up to this point, I thought I was pretty hot stuff, and I would argue with practically anyone about anything. My mother used to say I should become a lawyer! But suddenly I was confronted with something I couldn't argue with. Being hot stuff was terribly bad.

So there I was, at the tender age of eleven, and what the girls thought of me would not become monumentally important for another couple of years. And yet, those girls were the messengers of some very deflating news. To this day, I still remember looking at my page in the slam book, thinking, "There's something wrong with me. There's something wrong with being really good at things, being expressive, being 'big!'" In that instant, I placed a bubble around myself to keep me from being too "big," to keep me from being judged as conceited by the girls. I took on the weight of their judgment and lugged it around for over two decades. And in every relationship I entered, I imagined that my partner was watching and waiting for me to be "too big" so she could judge me as conceited and embarrass me, making her own entry in the slam book. I blamed my partner for keeping me inside my bubble.

I am still learning to allow myself to be really "big." I understand that, at eleven, I was pretty self-absorbed. The girls probably would have loved to be able to connect with me more, but I wasn't available. At least, that's my perception of the situation now. The important thing is that I have been able to forgive the girls for judging me as conceited, and I have been able to release my judgment of myself. By releasing the weight of that judgment, I now see my free expression and enthusiasm as blessings to myself and my relationships. The bubble is almost gone.

This is why awareness is so important. As we become more aware of what is, who we are, who our partners are, and how our past colors our present, we "gain altitude" and see more clearly the order and sense of our experience. We move closer to the Divine view of things. This can be a very powerful experience, and often when it occurs we experience spontaneous forgiveness of self and others, followed by great peace and joy.

This also works well in healing our relationships with our parents. Whether our parents are alive or not, we carry our birth family with all its history inside us. Major relationship challenges often result from our unconscious attempts to re-create familiar, emotionally charged scenes from our family past. Imagine witnessing and reviewing your father's or mother's life from an altitude. Can you see how it might make sense that they were the way they were? Can you find compassion and forgiveness there? As you release any anger, resentment, or judgment you may have on your parents, you will see change in the landscape of your current relationship.

So, before you attempt to change the thing you judge most about yourself or your partner in relationship, first study it. Invite it up from the shadowy basement into your living room. Offer it a cup of tea. It is your teacher. As you move into non-judgmental awareness of what is at Point A, you begin to free yourself to move toward Point B, the way you would rather it be.

VISION

"The soul never thinks without a picture."
Aristotle

"Your imagination is your preview of life's coming attractions."
Albert Einstein

With clear awareness you can have clear vision. In the early stages of working with a couple, I make sure and give them a while to complain, so long as it does not become attacking. I believe it is important to let the complaint "tape" run for a while so that the person feels heard. At some point, though, I find it natural to ask, "How do you want it to be?" "Well," they might say, "I want him to stop complaining." "I want her to stop spending so much money." There is so much attention focused upon the "problems" that they have practically lost all vision of the positive way of being they desire.

But what you resist, persists. This seems to be one of the big unwritten rules of the world. Whatever you focus your mind's energy upon tends to move to the foreground. You will be less successful by trying to move away from what you don't want. You will be more successful by focusing your attention toward the way you want your relationship to be – your forward vision.

Shift your attention away from what you want your partner to change. Changing your partner is a pretty futile mission anyway. Shift your vision toward the loving relationship that you wish to create together. This is your relationship Point B. The more clearly and vividly you can imagine Point B, the more likely you are to get there.

One very powerful way to assist in manifesting your vision is to write it down. Do this separately, then get together and collaborate on a joint version, and follow these rules:

1. Describe your relationship as you wish it to be, in rich and vivid detail, using lots of colorful and juicy adjectives.
2. Write it in present tense, as if you are experiencing it right now.
3. Use all positive language, talk about it being the way you want it rather than not being the way you don't want it. For example, instead of "Our arguments never get out of control," say, "We handle our disagreements consciously and responsibly."
4. Describe your relationship on several levels, feelings, thoughts, and any material/physical details, again in vivid detail.
5. Be as specific as you want to be, but do not describe the process of how to get from where you are to Point B. Write as if it has already happened.
6. You can make it a "stretch," but make it believable.
7. If there are any pictures or images you can draw or cut from magazines that visually represent your ideal scene, include those.
8. Write it with the understanding that it will be happening at some fixed point in the future, say 6 months or 1 year.

You can review it often, or put it away until it's time. Some couples do this every New Year to be opened at Thanksgiving, an opportunity to express gratitude for what has come to be, and gratitude for the lessons and opportunities inherent in what perhaps did not come true. See the back of this book for examples of actual written visions.

While opinions vary regarding whether or how this works, I am convinced that it does indeed work very powerfully because I have seen it work in my life many times, and I have seen it work consistently in the lives of those with whom I work. We know that what we say to ourselves – our "self talk" – is important. What we focus our mind's energy on is more likely to manifest. Many self-help books and workshops teach this as a practice of the conscious mind that yields more desired results in our lives.

But there also seems to be something else going on. Your unconscious mind is listening to what you say. It is listening and responding, "As you wish." In fact, it is your unconscious mind saying, "As you wish" that may have led you to develop beliefs when you were young, beliefs that don't work for you now. You may have come to believe things such as, "I'll never do well in school. I'm a failure. I'm not worthy of being loved. Men leave. Women lie. Money is scarce." Your unconscious mind may be carrying such messages and playing them back to you now, but it is also listening for new messages.

So by providing a vivid, present tense, written description of your relationship "ideal scene" you are painting a picture for your unconscious mind, sending it a message that this is the way it is. As you wish.

On a spiritual level, I would propose that it is also possible that a greater Divine power is also listening and saying, "As you wish." It seems that the unconscious mind is a very effective link to that greater power. There is much recent scientific evidence as to the existence of collective unconscious and collective consciousness. Your written vision may access the greater power of the collective.

So if this is such a great tool, why doesn't it always work? Opinions vary on this as well, and a full discussion is beyond the scope of this book. A simple explanation may be as follows. Consider for a moment that there is a higher plan for your life, for your soul's growth, and for those around you. Your written vision is like a prayer that your conscious mind makes. If it is in alignment with the higher plan, you will move quickly toward it. If it conflicts, you may not. But your prayers do seem to have force and effect in the Divine equation. They make a difference.

If your written vision does not move you toward your ideal scene, it is likely to move you toward *something*. If this happens, consider the possibility that you are being shown an opportunity or a lesson. As you declare your vision and move forward, you are likely to encounter all the "Yeah, but…s" lurking in the shadows. One big clue that this is the case is if the *something*, the obstacle, keeps happening again and again, and you are very upset, angry, or in judgment about it.

This often happens. Something appears that looks as if it is in your way. It doesn't look anything like what you've asked for. The very thing that seems in your way might be part of "the way," the path to Point B. Perhaps Point B is in alignment with the higher plan, but there's something you need to first address, heal, or learn as part of your soul's growth. Wonder about the thing or the person that appears to be in your way. It could be another teacher.

Sometimes the written vision process hits a "dead end." I think one of the difficult things to know is when I need to learn from the obstacle or if it is telling me that, no matter what I learn, this path is somehow not in the cards for me. One clue to this seems to be my level of upset. If I am "upset because..." it is likely that I still have something to learn about this situation. But if I have equanimity, non-judgment, and compassion about it, then the lesson may be to surrender this path and seek another path, or to modify the vision.

Whether or not you use the written process, know that it is important for you to get clear about how you want things to be, clearly see your target before you take action.

ACTION

"I define love thus: The will to extend one's self for the purpose of nurturing one's own or another's spiritual growth."
    M. Scott Peck, M.D., from "The Road Less Traveled"

In the above quote, love is defined as "the will to extend..." These words conjure up images of reaching out, of taking action in relationship with another. I like this because it takes love out of the dreamy blue sky and puts it right in the living room. Dr. Peck is telling us that *loving is a verb.* As time goes on I find myself talking less about love and more about loving. The ideas presented here – to forgive, tell the truth, take full responsibility, and commit – represent loving in action.

We usually think of action steps as outer actions, such as buying her flowers once a month, telling him how much you appreciate him once a week, telling her you love her every day, and so on. The important action steps in relationships are more inner actions. The inner actions will naturally yield all those outer actions, and you will experience them from a much deeper level of authenticity and loving.

As you move into non-judgmental awareness and clear forward vision, your life and relationship may automatically begin to shift to align with your vision. No overt action seems necessary. This is one of the ways grace works in our lives. But give yourself some credit. If you find yourself in non-judgmental awareness, you may have already taken inner action, because moving into non-judgment requires the act of forgiveness.

FORGIVE

"Two Buddhist monks, on their way to the monastery, found an exceedingly beautiful woman at the riverbank. Like them, she wished to cross the river, but the water was too high. So one of the monks lifted her onto his back and carried her across. His fellow monk was thoroughly scandalized. For two hours he berated him on his negligence in keeping the rule: Had he forgotten he was a monk? How did he dare touch a woman? And worse, carry her across the river? What would

people say? Had he brought their holy religion into disrepute? The offending monk listened patiently to the neverending sermon. Finally he broke in and said, 'Brother, I left that woman at the river. Are you still carrying her?'"
Anonymous

Forgiveness is not about letting someone off the hook. Forgiveness is not about forgetting. Forgiveness is compassion in action. As you reach higher levels of awareness, higher altitudes, compassionate forgiveness often happens spontaneously. If not, it can be facilitated through therapy or other techniques.

Forgiveness is something you do for *you*. It requires a willingness to get off your position, to move on. It is a freeing act that you know when it has worked because you feel an increased sense of peace, relief, lightness, and energy. You have released the weight of judgment.

Your forgiveness job isn't over when you have forgiven others. How do you know when you have an opportunity to forgive yourself? Any time you find yourself pointing a finger at someone else, saying "I'm upset with you because..." odds are good that you have such an opportunity. Your upset is a clue that there is likely a part of yourself that looks just like the target of your upset. You have judged this part of yourself, pushed it into the shadows because you don't like it, and it becomes part of your unconscious. You project it onto others because your conscious mind denies that you could be "like that." Are you willing to look in the mirror? Are you willing to tell the uncomfortable truth that part of you is "like that?"

Perhaps you are upset because your partner is deceitful. If you can find the deceitful part in yourself, your task is to compassionately forgive yourself for judging yourself as deceitful, forgive yourself for judging your deceit as bad. This does not mean that it is okay to allow deceit in your relationship. You can make a commitment to the truth without being upset about it. Your odds of success are much greater if you can calmly state, "I am not willing to be at the effect of your deceit," rather than "I'm upset because you are deceiving me."

Sometimes it is difficult to get clear on just what your judgments are, and some practice or guidance may be needed to get to the root of it. You might find that what you initially thought you were judging is not it at all. You might find that your judgment of someone else is actually a judgment of yourself. Then you might find a deeper level of judgment beneath that. I have found that the core issue beneath so many judgments is a judgment of ourselves as *not worthy of our own loving*. This is a gigantic clue. Look deeply at your judgments. Is this true for you? If so, you now have the blessed opportunity to heal at the core level. Your mission is to first bring awareness to how it got set up this way. How did I decide I was not worthy of my own loving? Who gave me that message? Once you have altitude and can see the sense of it, you can speak the following magic words with compassion:

"I forgive myself for judging myself as unworthy of my own loving."

You are infinitely worthy of your own loving, and the loving of your partner. Believing anything else is a mistake.

TELL THE TRUTH

"You shall know the truth, and the truth shall make you free."
  John 8:32

Telling the truth is not about being "brutally honest." It does not give you permission to carelessly blurt out anything you might be thinking, no matter how negative, about your partner or someone else. The goal in telling the truth is to communicate what is true *for you* in the moment, authentically and with care.

Being honest with your partner goes to the very core of the quality of your relationship because without honesty you have no trust. Without trust do you really have a relationship? It's on shaky ground at best. So while being honest with your partner is important, telling the truth in relationship goes beyond that. It includes saying what's true for you in the moment, especially what you are feeling. Speaking your authentic truth can be your most effective tool for stopping arguments and for creating more intimacy.

We get locked into argument and conflict out of fear and out of the habit of our stories. We are doing the Waltz of the Victim, dancing in and out of the roles of Victim, Persecutor, and Rescuer. You may have a favorite role where you spend more time, but it is likely that you find yourself in the other two roles as well at times.

Stepping out of the dance requires you to first be aware that you are doing the dance. Bring your non-judgmental awareness to your own unique way of doing that dance.

Whichever role you prefer, wonder how it got set up that way. Is there anything to forgive or release judgment from? Stepping out of the dance requires a willingness to get off your position. One effective way to do this is to stop talking, take a deep breath or two, and ask yourself what is true for you right now, what is present. Pay especially close attention to your feelings and any body sensations.

See the back of the book for a list of "What's So" Questions and a Telling the Truth exercise that will help invite your awareness of what is true for you in the moment. You will know when you are doing this correctly because the argument or conflict will almost always stop cold. You have spoken the unarguable truth. Your truth will also carry the power of confession, which naturally invites your partner to come closer.

TAKE FULL RESPONSIBILITY

"If we become conscious of and stop the projections we make on each other, we can go a long way toward preventing the careless wounding we inflict on others as well as ourselves... So much suffering...stems from the deep resentments generated by lack of recognition between those who use each other as a screen upon which to project their own shadows."
Jean Houston, from "A Mythic Life"

Carl Jung spoke of responsibility as the "ability to respond." I believe that we acquire the ability to respond as we practice non-judgmental awareness. That is, the more aware we are of what is happening right now, the better we are able to respond to it. For our purposes, taking full responsibility goes beyond simply the ability to respond. It has to do with the quality or value of your response.

Taking full responsibility has many aspects. It includes doing what you say you are going to do, completing what you start, being on-time, and "walking your talk." *The quality of your life and your relationships is directly related to how fully you take responsibility.* Full responsibility also means "owning your own feelings." You are responsible for your own feelings. You are not responsible for your partner's. This may sound radical at first. I know it did to me when I first learned it. But it is very freeing.

One example of this occurred in my work with a couple in which she was very upset that he always complained and scolded her. He agreed that he complained a lot, and felt justified. After working with him a few sessions, he decided that he was "a man who no longer complained." However, the next time she came in with him, she claimed he was complaining and "scolding" more than ever! Her use of the word "scold" was a clue. When she spoke of it, I sensed a part of her that was very young. And at one point, she admitted that she felt I was scolding her, that she had done something wrong and she didn't know what it was.

Once she was able to take responsibility for her upset and wonder how it got set up that way, she was able to discover that her feeling of being scolded and not knowing why came from her early experiences with her father. We then worked to heal her relationship with her father, after which she freed herself of the need to see her husband as "scolding." Only when she was able to see herself as no longer a victim of her father's scolding was she able to see her husband as someone who does not scold.

Some people, when I propose that they are not responsible for their partner's feelings, say, "Well, if I'm not responsible for my partner's feelings, I guess that means I can do or say anything I want and not worry about hurting their feelings. Right?" No. First of all, if you do or say anything you want without regard for your partner, you are demonstrating a lack of integrity and commitment to the relationship. It is useless to talk about responsibility if commitment and integrity are absent.

Second, when I hear someone talk about hurting another's feelings or getting his or her feelings hurt, I know this person is almost always doing the Waltz of the Victim. "Hurt" is not an emotion. Hurt implies that someone is inflicting pain and someone is experiencing the pain. Our emotional response to this is usually sadness and/or anger. Instead of saying, "You hurt my feelings" try saying, "I'm sad (or angry)." Energetically, this moves you from the victim role into responsibility for your feelings. From that place you can then proclaim, "This does not work for me."

Any time your finger is pointing outside yourself and you hear yourself saying some version of, "I'm upset because..." you have an opportunity to take responsibility for your own upset. Notice it, wonder about it, tell the truth about it. Is there an opportunity for forgiveness of self or others, for release of judgment?

People talk about codependency. Codependency is what happens when you are not taking full responsibility. If you are in the Victim role you are taking less than full responsibility, you require a Rescuer to make you complete. But while this is going on there is a part of you that resents your Rescuer for not acknowledging and honoring you as a whole human being. So you step into the Persecutor role. Meanwhile, the Rescuer is taking more than full responsibility, and does not feel whole unless there is a Victim to take care of. This is a "one-up" position that also finds the Rescuer naturally stepping into the Persecutor role. And don't be surprised if the Rescuer starts feeling like a Victim when his or her partner steps from the Victim into the Persecutor role. It is a dizzying dance.

I invite you to remove the word codependency from your vocabulary. Replace it with full responsibility, the thing you want to move toward.

Please understand that I am not suggesting that you *always* tell the truth and *always* take full responsibility. That is impossible. What I am suggesting is that you consider a commitment to truth and responsibility as guiding principles. The more you practice them, the more aware you become of when you are out of alignment with them. It's like the autopilot in an airplane. With practice you will stop crashing into mountains and stay closer to the course of truth and responsibility. And know that the times you find yourself off-course are when you will find the opportunities to grow and evolve your self and your relationship.

"Fear not this love, for it is Divinely given.
It offers an open heart, not a desperate grasp at your
freedom."
    Soji

Commitment is about truly *being in* the relationship. If there are major issues to work out, consider committing to staying in the relationship – no matter what (except for abuse) – for a specified length of time, say six months to a year. This helps avoid the "back door problem" that happens frequently when relationships get challenging. Things start getting uncomfortable and one of you says, "I'm leaving!" This often happens when someone is about to face something uncomfortable. I refer to this pattern as having one's "psychic bags packed at the door." Issues can slosh around unresolved forever in this state.

Notice that what we are talking about is a commitment to a process, the process of being present in the moment, with awareness of what is, telling the truth, and living in full responsibility. This is different from commitment to a future event or outcome, which is what people often mean when they talk about commitment in relationship.

For example, most marriage vows are about commitments to outcomes, promises to be a certain way until death. The problem is, you don't know how you are going to feel tomorrow. And often, the morning after the wedding, you may be having some new feelings that you do not know what to do with. If both of you have a commitment to be fully in the relationship and speak your truth, then you have a safe space where you can openly explore these new feelings. You can admit that you're scared or you feel vulnerable. If you don't have that space, where do the feelings go? They hide in the basement of your mind, gaining strength, waiting to come splurting out some time later.

So, while commitments to outcomes may be wonderful, they seem to work best when accompanied with commitments to the process of showing up, staying in, and telling your truth. Use these "process commitments" to create that safe space for each of you to say what's true.

You have a right to a relationship committed to truth and full responsibility, if that is what you want. Once you both agree to this commitment and begin to practice telling the truth and taking full responsibility, you will experience much greater closeness. Perhaps you will feel lighter, more energetic. Every untold truth that is spoken and taken responsibility for will discharge some "static" that has been between you, that has been confounding your communications and blocking your intimacy. You will be creating a clear space between you through which the energy of loving will surge and flow. You become more spontaneous and creative, individually and together.

When you begin experiencing this loving, creative flow, you may wish to consider another commitment. That is, a commitment to support and nurture each other's creative expression. Not only have you reached your relationship Point B, but your relationship now becomes a gift that others can share as they experience your loving and creative expression.

So when you reach this point, have you graduated? No. You do not graduate from Relationship School, but if you keep showing up for the lessons, it just gets better. You get fewer lessons and more celebration! To the extent you are willing, your relationship can be a rich vehicle for self discovery and soul evolution. The relationship dance invites you into ever-deeper levels of knowing each other and yourself. As you shed the layers of pretense, projection, and fear, you just may find yourself spending more time in spontaneous gratitude and joy. How much are you willing to receive?

One of my dearest friends and teachers, Cheryl Medicine Song, wrote a rich and powerful piece that deeply touched me, "On Partnership." She was inspired to write it when her partner in conscious relationship asked her, "Just what does partnership mean to you?" Her partner expected a simple answer, but this is what came back. I share this passage with you now, and invite you to find inspiration in these words, with blessings and wishes of grace in your relationship's journey.

ON PARTNERSHIP

The joining of two spirits and bodies for the divine unfolding and ongoing re-creation of each individual's soul and life path...

With its primary focus being to support, love, hold, set free, bring close again, honestly witness and lovingly challenge one's beloved and one's self...

Offering each other a heart-based nest of love for the other to come home to and rest in, a place in which they can fully be themselves...

Offering an honest light that gently, yet pointedly challenges one's beloved to become her very best, to leave no discovered stone unturned...

And offering a mirror that reflects all that the other is: the shadow and the illumined, the limitations and the masteries, the grief and the joys...

Making room to celebrate it all, to honor it all, to bathe every discovered dark crevice in the light of brilliant, radiant, soothing love...

Partnership offers a love that is mature and unconditional, where each one cares for their own soul's growth and where each one says to the other, "I am here loving you. I am your beloved no matter who shows up today, no matter what part of yourself is discovered and left naked, and no matter what part of your intricate self remains a mystery for now."

Partnership offers to each other a love that is absolutely unrelenting in its invitation to "show up," to really show up in all one's glory and in all one's wretchedness, to dare to hide nothing at all. It is a love that is equally unrelenting in its invitation to dream and to grow and to breathe and to fly, even if the taking flight takes one's beloved away. And yet it is a love that also considers the "we" before taking flight, attending with care to the launching pad you've both created, to the wings and the wind that make taking flight even possible.

Partnership attends to love's holy temple, to the sacred energy and light of the "we," with regular attention and prayer, releasing self-centeredness long enough each day to notice and attend to the needs of one's beloved, the needs they have so courageously allowed to be seen...and then to speak to one's beloved with the words and wisdom and love utterances that one's beloved's heart and soul long to hear, need to hear, in order to help them remember their preciousness, their unique place in this web of Life, their inseparable oneness with God.

Partnership offers the space for unique, individual creation and expression; offers room to dance and sing and stand alone...honors the unique, "different-than-one's-self" being of the other...applauds her song...understands her need to sometimes solitarily create her own universe, again and again and again...and is willing to ask with interest again and again, "So who are you?" and opens one's mind and heart to the ever-changing answers.

Partnership is a commitment to touch one's beloved...to care for the physical, sensual body of the other, that physical temple of Divine Spirit...to care for each body with tenderness and respect and reverence and knowing and curiosity and interest and passion and delight...to regularly enter into the ecstatic union with each other and with Spirit that you came together to know and to create, allowing your erotic love to discover and re-discover the many entry-ways, gateways to the Temple, the many sanctuaries and altars waiting to be adorned with the love and desire that dances between the two of you.

Partnership is a moving, permeable energy that is solid enough to take root in and fluid enough to flow with the changes, the many truths of time and personal evolution. And in all its longing to finally arrive home, partnership is still courageous enough and patient enough and willing enough to witness and embrace the mystery of love...the mysterious, unknown, sometimes lonely void that takes shape deep in the rich and expansive heart of love...and to embrace life and death hand-in-hand, again and again, as you walk hand-in-hand, again and again.

© 1999, Cheryl Medicine Song

APPENDICES

BASIC COMMUNICATION SKILL – HEART
CENTERED LISTENING

"WHAT'S SO" QUESTIONS – THE PATH TO
UNARGUABLE TRUTH

TELLING THE TRUTH EXERCISE

EXAMPLES OF RELATIONSHIP VISIONS

BASIC COMMUNICATION SKILL
HEART CENTERED LISTENING

"One true self speaks to another, using the language of the heart, and in that bond a person is healed." Deepak Chopra, Unconditional Life

The purpose of this skill is to develop a way of communicating that honors the person with whom you are talking. One of the most loving things you can offer your partner is your full understanding of what they are saying.

Some Native Americans have a ritual called the Talking Circle. While sitting in circle, a Talking Stick is passed. While the person holding the Talking Stick speaks, all others are silent, honoring the speaker.

Get yourself a Talking Stick! It could actually be a stick, or it could be some other object that has special meaning. Sit facing each other, one of you hold the Talking Stick, and speak while the other sits in silence. The speaker's job is to speak the unarguable truth, no more than about three thoughts at a time, or about a minute's worth. The listener's job is to listen from the heart, fully attending to what the speaker is saying. If you find yourself beginning to formulate a response, argument, or comeback, just let that go and return your full attention to the speaker. The listener may notice thoughts, feelings, or body sensations, but should wait to express them until they have the Talking Stick.

When the Talking Stick is passed, the new speaker's first job is to tell your partner what you heard them say, as accurately as you can, without adding your own interpretation. Use these words, "What I heard you say was…Is that accurate?" If the answer is yes, the new speaker then takes his or her turn. If the answer is no, or not quite, pass the Talking Stick back for clarification. Then try again, "What I heard you say was…Is that accurate?" Continue until the speaker feels completely heard and understood.

Once you become proficient at this you will find yourselves naturally honoring each other more in your everyday communications. Use this skill any time either of you feels challenged in fully communicating something or being fully understood.

"WHAT'S SO" QUESTIONS THE PATH TO UNARGUABLE TRUTH

What am I feeling?

　　Anger, sadness, joy, or fear

How am I experiencing this in my body?

What judgments am I making on myself or another?

Am I willing to look for the learning opportunity here?

What is my real intention?

What outcome do I want? (Turn your complaint into a request.)

How is this familiar? (How is my past coloring my present?)

What might I be gaining by holding onto my position?

What role am I playing in my story?

   Victim, persecutor, rescuer

What am I responsible for? What am I not responsible for?

Telling the Truth

The purpose of this exercise is to practice noticing and reporting what is true for you in each moment. Your skill at this will be useful in times of upset or disagreement with your partner, and will help facilitate your moving out of the Waltz of the Victim into the unarguable truth.

This exercise may be practiced alone or with a partner. Sit comfortably in a quiet place where you will not be disturbed. Sit upright and in an open body position, with both feet on the floor. You may close your eyes or leave them open. Perhaps you will want to try it both ways to see which works better for you.

1. Begin by taking six slow, deep, full breaths, allowing your abdominal area to expand and contract effortlessly.
2. Next, your partner asks, or you ask yourself silently, "What's present right now?"
3. Answer this question by simply stating what is true in the moment. It can be a thought, an emotion, or a body sensation. There is no right or wrong answer, only what is true right now. Just a few words should suffice.
4. Go back into silence, take three or four slow, deep breaths, and repeat the question, "What's present right now?"

5. Answer the question again, reporting whatever is true for you right now.
6. Repeat this process at least ten times. You can do more than ten times if needed to be complete.
7. Pay special attention to body sensations and emotions. They tend to keep us present in the moment, whereas our thoughts often take us out of the moment.
8. If you or your partner notice your thoughts taking you out of the moment, perhaps telling a story about…something, simply notice that and gently and compassionately bring your awareness back to the present moment. What's present right now?
9. If you are doing this with a partner, change partners and repeat. Once you are both complete, share anything that you noticed or learned. It may be profound, or it may be nothing. Whatever it is, allow your experience to be okay just as it is. There is no right or wrong result.

EXAMPLES OF RELATIONSHIP VISIONS

Example 1: An almost-newlywed couple

To be opened on Thanksgiving Day:
We are grateful for so many things. We are experiencing life flowing with grace and ease. We have opened up to an abundance of loving that we never thought possible, and we continue to raise our upper limits as to how much loving we give and receive. We are aware of the presence of Spirit in and around us, in all things. We continue to heal our illusions of separateness from Spirit. We meditate almost every day. Our sanctuary is filled with blessed energy so that anyone who enters experiences healing. We are candles shining on the earthly plane. We are light and energetic, and we are having lots of fun.

We are joyously married. The wedding was glorious, a heart-opening experience for us and everyone there. Our hearts are filled with love for each other. We are definitely enrolled in relationship school, learning with grace and ease from each other, from our relationship, and having lots of fun in the process. We inspire each other to be our best. We have a new beautiful baby that keeps us busy and continually melts our hearts. The child is vibrant and healthy, and is already a shining inspiration to those around us. Even with all this going on, we enjoy lots of music, fun events, and a fun getaway trip or two.

We are physically healthy, exercise regularly, and our diet supports our continued health and high energy. We spend lots of time outside, in nature.

We are continuing to experience healing of family relationships and increasing awareness of family patterns. Our families continue to be healthy and well. We are more whole, wise, and loving as a result of our individual work with our teachers, and we bring this wholeness, wisdom and loving into the relationship where it thrives. We are showing up fully in every moment.

We are grateful for the close friends we have and the new ones we are making. We enrich each other, laugh a lot, and learn a lot.

We are enjoying our work as an opportunity to serve and work with people where there is truly a need. We feel fulfilled and deeply grateful to be able to do this work.

We are enjoying the beauty of the garden more and more, spending at least one day a week on average in the garden. It continues to be a metaphor for our lives and relationship, as we experience a natural unfolding of great abundance and beauty.

And so it is!

Example 2: A single woman ready for a new relationship

My life companion personifies love and friendship. He participates in the fullness of life with me and eagerly welcomes the adventure of our every day together. He revels in being with me and I delight in his presence. He feels and demonstrates great pleasure in our life together. We are an exquisite match.

This man appreciates family. He honors the relationships I have with my children and family. My children like him. He has his own children who adore him and appreciate his opinion.

Physically, we take good care of ourselves, enjoy regular workouts at the gym, go skiing each season, we cycle, hike, backpack, and run. We love to spend hours at the beach or by a pool. He enjoys nude sunbathing as much as I do. We enjoy foods of all kinds, all cultures. Eating is actually an adventure for us.

Our sexual relationship is exotic, erotic, sensual, loving, connected, and varied. We communicate before, during and after lovemaking. With loving, touching, affection, talking, laughing, our hearts are linked. This link translates into a spiritual experience with our loving. My man delights in giving and receiving affection. We spend evenings close to each other touching toes or fingers while we are curled on the couch reading. People can tell we like being with each other. He displays caring and warmth for me in front of the kids. I enjoy walking past him and planting a kiss on his cheek. The smile I get is delightful.

His smile is endless, demonstrating his deep inner peace. He is positive and serene. He knows himself. He likes the man that he is. His smile is especially inviting over a glass of wine while we are chatting and watching a sunset. He is most handsome when he smiles. His self-confidence is quietly apparent. He has impeccable honesty. Even when it is difficult, he values honesty above protection.

We LOVE MUSIC!!! YEAH!!! We share the deep joys of a wide variety of music. Our life together is surrounded by music and we attend concerts of all kinds. We are both engaged in successful, profitable business, we love our work.

We travel lots, running around the countryside in our car or on the back of his motorcycle. My man and I love to play in the sand, climb rocks, sip fine wine, watch movies, share tales with friends, travel to new places, make love, shop, explore museums, read to kids, meditate, and swing on swings.

ABOUT THE AUTHOR:

Richard Jordan was born and raised in rural Missouri and now lives in California. Richard combines his experience in psychology, spirituality, and environmental sciences in service to individuals and groups interested in conscious evolution. He especially enjoys working with couples to bring more loving into their relationships. He has a Masters Degree in Spiritual Psychology and a Doctorate in Clinical Psychology. He also has extensive business experience in major corporate management as well as having started, built, and sold a successful environmental services firm.

Richard studies and practices Eastern philosophy and meditation techniques, various forms of Yoga, and rituals and customs of indigenous cultures; weaving these various wisdom traditions into his work. He has also learned much about life from his garden.

✍ Notes ✍

Order Form

To order additional copies, fill out this form and send it along with your check or money order to: Dr. Richard Jordan, 219 Broadway, #291, Laguna Beach, CA 92651.

Cost per copy $12.00 plus $4.00 P&H. If shipped to an address in California, add $0.93 for state sales tax for each book.

Ship _____ copies of *Relationship School: A Path of Conscious Loving* to:

Name_____

Address:_____

Address:_____

Address:_____

❑   **Check box for signed copy**